CUTE CHRISTMAS
COLORING BOOK

PRO TIP!
When using wet mediums such as markers, place a blank sheet of paper behind the coloring page to prevent bleed-through.

THANK YOU FOR YOUR PURCHASE!

TEST YOUR COLOR

TEST YOUR COLOR

TEST YOUR COLOR

Made in the USA
Columbia, SC
29 October 2024